The Purple Book
A book of poetry
Written by: Cleo Kaine

The Lil Diva copy — mommy love you — Cleo Kaine

Books purchased with a dull or missing cover are most likely stolen and unauthorized by publisher. Please notify publisher immediately of where and when you purchased the illegal copy.

Published by
Purple Publication
P O Box 1986
Pine Bluff, Arkansas 71613
www.facebook.com/purplepublicationllc

Copyright ©2017 Cleo Kaine
All rights reserved
ISBN-13: 978-147833073
ISBN-10: 1478330074

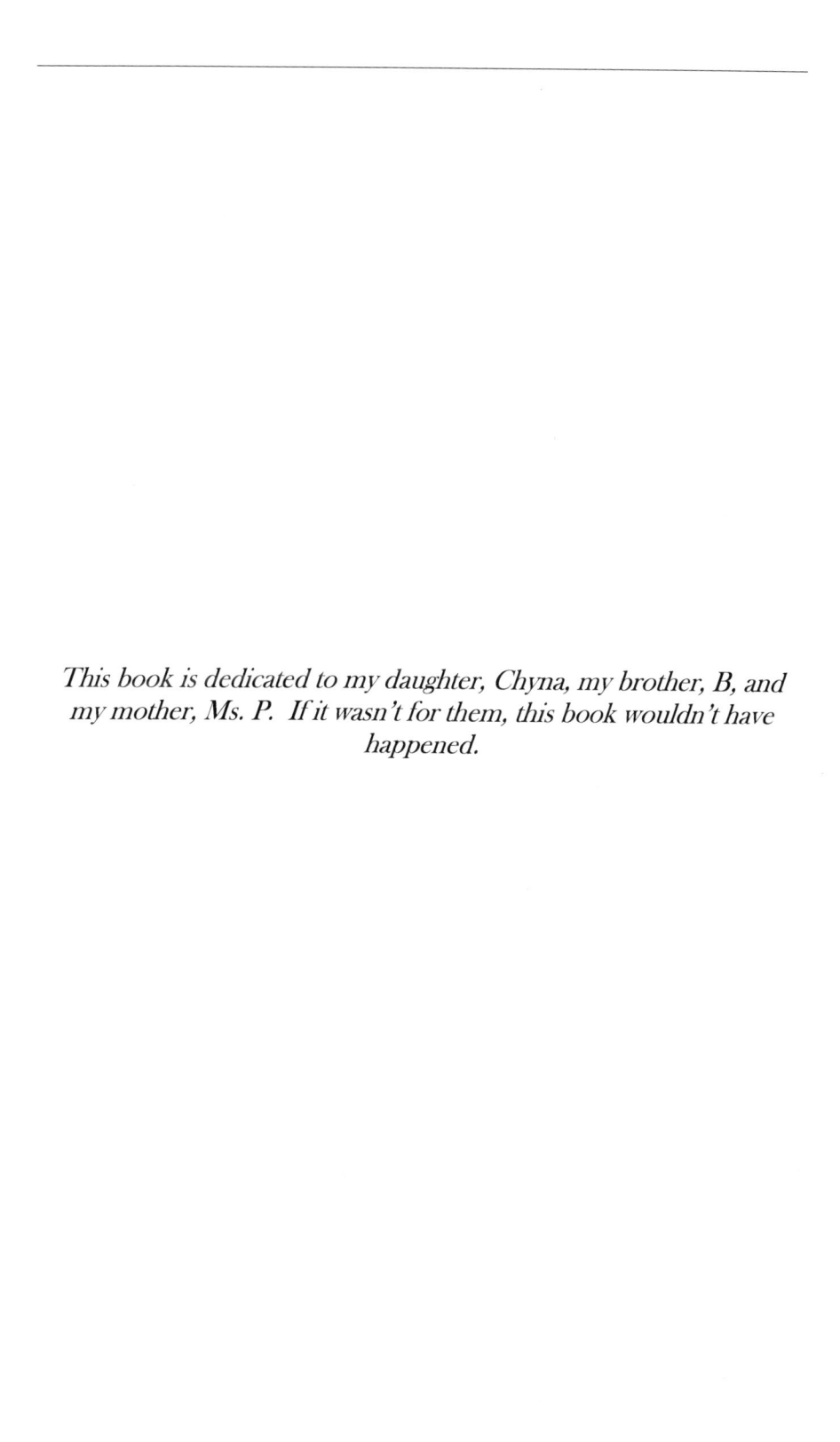

This book is dedicated to my daughter, Chyna, my brother, B, and my mother, Ms. P. If it wasn't for them, this book wouldn't have happened.

My Purple Rainbow

I am here
Looking at my purple rainbow
With all the shades of purple
I see the deep and brightness of the hues
Sparkling with hopes and riches
Some may call it mysterious
I turn to see the lighter shades
That glow with romance
And splattered with lilac, lavender and orchid flowers
The redder the purple
The warmer the world is
The bluer the purple
The cooler the water
My purple rainbow
Is my favorite rainbow of all

Love Prayer

Let God bless this love
And let these two lovers
Be together forever
God please guide them
To the right road of love
Through the good and the bad times
Let them be together
As eternal soul mates
To be together forever
In the name of the Father, the Son and the Holy Ghost
Amen

I am a Pretty Girl

I am a pretty girl
With some pretty curls
That bounces with every ounce
Of my behind
I am a pretty girl
In a pretty girl's world
Which have haters
That doesn't want to be a team player
And participate in the game
I am pretty girl
With a pretty good head
That no one can steal
Very smart, never dumb
Make people wonder
What a pretty girl thinks
I am a pretty girl
In a pretty mind, body and soul
Don't you want to be a pretty girl too

Forever Gone

He is forever gone
Forever out of my life
Why?
I asked myself millions of times
Maybe he found someone else better
I tell myself over and over again
But t can't be that he is gone forever
Why do I keep on thinking about him day and night?
In my mind, I know he will never come back
But I wonder how you tell your broken heart
Sometimes I try to forget he exists
It doesn't work
He is never coming back
I wonder does he think about me
He said that he would never forget about me
I believe he has
He hasn't written nor called to say, "Hi"
He really doesn't love me any more
I found the perfect guy at one time in my life
But he left me with shatter dreams and hopes
That we would be together forever

Big Brother

I always looked up to you
For advice that I needed
You seem to have the answers
I tried to help you
And wouldn't let me
But whenever you could
You tried to help me
We used to sit up all night
And talk about anything
Now that you are gone
I don't have anyone to talk to
I miss you very much
And I will never forget
You will always be in my heart

Being Blessed

It is funny how we look up to God
When we don't have anything
But soon as the good life comes
We forget to thank him for what he has given us
We stop going to church every Sunday like we use to
We stop paying our tithes and start investing in good time
Some people don't know that you can have a good time at church
Just as well as a club
Sometimes we wonder why the Lord blesses us with
Just enough to get by
Some people don't know that greed is a sin
To be blessed is just enough
To be greedy is too much
So, do you think he is asking for too much
It won't hurt just for you to praise him
And give him thanks for what you have

Freedom

Freedom is a key that holds our future
It something everybody gains
Because they did something wrong
It takes them a long time to gain this key back
It takes others a short amount of time
Some people never find the key
So, don't lose the key to freedom

Letter to Child

March 19, 1993

To My Dear Sweet Child,

    I know I probably will not get a chance to see you come into this cruel world. I think there are some things that I should tell you about the world. As my child, you will go through some good and bad times. You will come in this world young and eager to learn. You will leave this world tired and full of wisdom. I hope that your generation will be the generation that solves the world's problems. Be brave and smart and you can do whatever you want to do in this world. I want you to know that I love you.

Love,
Mommy

The Vow

I vow to love you
No matter what
To be there for you mentally, spiritually and emotionally
I will never let anybody or thing
Get between us
I vow to stay
By your side
Through the good and bad
Even when you are sick
I will be nursing you back to health
I will be your back bone
To help you up
To be strong
I vow to be your lover
To satisfy you
In all ways necessary
I promise not to let you down
It is all yours to have
Anytime anyway anyplace
I vow to be devoted
Never leaving your side
I love you forever
Til death do us part

One Night

I remember a time
That you didn't want to go home
You wanted to spend the night
Hugged up with me
A time in which you had a full course meal
And you licked the plate clean
It hurts you to go home
To a woman that doesn't satisfy your
Mental, spiritual and physical well-being
To you she is more like a midnight snack
And not the full pack
When you close your eyes
You have visions of me
As you nibble on her
Thinking in your mind
That this doesn't feel as silky and smooth as me
You even made the mistake and call her my name
You close your eyes
Dreaming of that one night
That you will get another
Taste of a full course meal
And won't go home to a midnight snack

My Name is Anne

My name is Anne
I'm an abused child
My mother is an abused wife
My father is a druggie
When I was a baby
I use to cry
Then my father would get up
And hit me on the behind
When I was five
My mother took me
And we ran away
We were almost to Grandma's house
When my father found us
He beat my mother almost to death
When I was ten
I started to develop
Like all other girls
I was growing up
My father started to sexually abuse me
It was horrible
He told me if I told my mother
That he would kill me
So, I went and told a teacher
She didn't believe me
I told the principal
She believed me
She called my aunt
And told her what had happen
The police came and picked up my dad
And I never saw him again
My name is Anne
I'm a better person now
I put my past behind me
And look into the future
In which the present become the past
And I'm looking forward to a bigger
And brighter future

Wonder

Sometimes I wonder
What it would be like
To have a man to come home to
Sometimes I wonder
What it would be like
To get in the bed
With the one that you love
I lay in my bed wondering
How it would feel
To be warmly touched
In those places, again
Will he come home today?
Or tomorrow maybe
But until that time
I will be wondering

Painted Nails

When I paint my nail red
You tend to call
You claim you want to shoot the breeze
But you want me to perform a task for you
That I dare to not mention
When I don't paint my nails
You rather be with your boys instead
When I paint my nails blue
You put me on a pedestal
For everyone to admire
How beautiful I am
But when the paint wears off
You think that I'm too ugly
To be around
So, if I don't paint my nail today
That means it is over
Between me and you

I Use to

I use to love the way you talk
Hearing your sweet mellow voice
Makes me extremely moist
Your smooth lyric use to
Fill my heart with the warmth of your love
I use to love your touch
To feel your strong hands
All against my soft body
Especially how they touch me
When we kiss
All I hear is sweet love songs
For I use to love you
In a way, I still do

Dreams

I once had a dream of us being together as one
A dream that I use to dream very often
Dreams of us raising our family together
In precious harmony
A dream that we will grow old
And see our generations of offsprings
Grow up to be very successful in life
But you shattered this dream
By messing with my heart
Thinking that I am a fool
When you are around being a hoe
I sick and tires of my love
Being used and abused
By a man that don't deserve me
So as this sweet dream
Turn into a nightmare
I got to say goodbye to you forever

Purple Panties

I am standing here
Wearing those purple panties
That you love to see me in
You remember the lace ones
That holds the package
That you want to unwrap
I want to take you
To the depths
To which no one has been before
I want you to let me explore
Your treasure with my tongue
And I will let you play with the pearl in my box
Let me take you on a journey
To a place where there is only me and you
I want to ride you on cloud nine
Where we can make the sweetest love
That no one can define
Come embrace me
With those strong arms
Let our lips touch
So that our soul will become one
Before I let you
Remove the purple panties
Off your kitty
Will you please be gentle?
Now you may remove the panties

Alone

He looked so tender and sweet
As he walked away
A tear drop fell from his eye
He walked away from the cold park
He thought about her palm
He turned around warmly
She looks so calm and nice
He hoped that day for all the best
It came out to be the worst
Now he's all alone and hurt
And he feels like dirt

Baby Daddy

Always calling
Always talking
About what he is going to do for the baby
Not there for her when she needs him
Calling my phone all times of night
Hoping I answer so that he
Can get some tonight
He says that he is coming to see her
But he coming to see me
Thinking that he is going to get into my panties
Where are the pampers?
Where is the milk?
He says, 'I ain't got no money but can I get some tonight?'
Soon as I told him
I don't want him any more
He doesn't call to check on the baby
He disclaims her
And act as she doesn't exist
I guess he is
A sorry ass baby daddy

The Room

The blackness of a room
That I have been locked up for years
The door cracks open
And I see a bright light
This light shine in my face
What was out there?
It was a big yellow star
Shining so bright
I wasn't cold any more
At last I'm free!

Tyrone

I poured my heart out to you
But you choose to throw it out like trash
And not treasure it
I gave you my all
And you gave me nothing
But heartaches and pain
Love is not supposed to feel this way
I put meals on your table
And you just spit on them
Like they weren't good enough
You tell people that I treat you like a peasant
But I treated you like a king
And you treated me like your servant
That's only there to provide
For your every need
I never cheated on you
But you cheated on me with many
Of your hoes, tricks and sluts
You always told me
You don't trust no bitch
Well after being with you
I won't trust any sorry ass niggas either

Mirror

I look at myself in the mirror
What do I see
A little girl with big dreams
Of becoming a lawyer
I look in the mirror
And who do I see
An adolescent that think she is ugly
Going through her first change
Only if she knew
Someday she may be a beauty queen
I look at myself
And wonder who that is
A young lady who thinks she knows the world
But only just begun life as she knows it
Still in high school and pressured by her peers
To have sex, drink beer and smoke weed
But she keeps her head up
I look in the mirror
And see a college girl
So anxious to see
What the world has to offer her
Going to the frat party
Enjoying her new-found freedom
Still learning about the world
I look in the mirror
To see a grow woman
Who had been through life
And still living it

The Presentation of a Woman

Gentlemen, I present to you
Something that is God's greatest creation
It came from the rib of Adam
And been his companion ever since
Please, please gentlemen, hold your bids
Of course, you know of what I'm talking about
Someone that you can talk to
At all times of the night
Gentlemen, I present to you
Someone that you can depend on
That will be by your side
When all your other friends put you down
Your best friend may be jealous
About someone who is as precious as a diamond
Gentlemen, I present to you
Someone that will scratch your back
When you have an itch
Someone that stand by your every decision
That won't leave you in your time of need
Gentlemen, please hold your bid
When you need a good meal
It can be fixed within a card deal
Gentlemen, hold your applauses
For cannot take a pause
Have ever come home to a clean house?
I know you would like someone there
To greet you when you come home
From that long day's work
And to give you a massage
Not to have your slippers
Full of dog slob
Someone that will have your meal ready
And your house clean
After that great meal, you just ate
You sit down in front of the TV
Someone that will snuggle next to you
While you are watching basketball

And later on that night
Someone that can fulfill
All your wettest dreams
Gentlemen, I present to you
God's greatest creation
THE WOMAN

The Place

Going to a place in my mind
That gives me peace
And tranquility to find
I'm searching for a place
That can read
And not worry
About the noisy neighbors
I want to stay in a place
Where my thought is heard
And not overlooked by others
Is there such a place
I am willing to find out

Life

When we were born
We shed tears
We went to school
To find career
That suits our personalities
A butcher, a baker or maybe a candy maker
Are some of the things we may be
We worked twelve long years
So that we can walk across a stage
To enter a world
That is unknown
But many people call it life

The Saggin Swaggar Brotha Man

That saggin brotha
Thinks he has some swag
Only if he knew
He looks like trash
That saggin swaggar brotha
Braggin to his friends
About the trick he slept with last night
That saggin swaggar brotha
About to trip on his pants
Because they're sagging too low
Only if he knew
If he pulled up his pants
He would be a better man

The Burning Bed

I'm lying on the side of you
Looking at your sexy chocolate body
Thinking about all the good times we had
Sometimes I think I'm dreaming
I must pitch myself
To make sure that it is real
I am standing next to the bed
Wondering do you really love me
Because just got a call from another woman
Who says that you love her instead
How could you do this to me?
I ask myself repeatedly
I gave you my all
And you push me down
If you only knew
What I just did
The bed you are sleeping in
I soaked the sheets with gasoline
As light, this match
I say good bye for every

Making Love

I heard a whisper in the dark
"I love you," he said
I saw a cooper young man
Looking at me with his doggy brown eyes
"Let's make love," he whispers
As he played with my ear
That night, our souls connected
The louder we moaned and groaned
Just represent how much fun we were having
When it was all over
He would kiss me passionately
Then we will go into a temporary slumber

The Perfect Man

I finally found the perfect man
He is caring and warm
When I come home from a hard day's work
He prepares dinner for me
He gives me fresh long stem roses when I'm sad
I know when he is coming
Because I smell the sweet fragrance of his cologne a mile away
He is always buying me something
Just the other day
He bought me expense French perfume
He compliments me on how I look
He said that Helen of Troy launched a thousand ships
But your beauty can bring them back home
I must be cursed
I gave him my heart
And he what does he do
He leaves

Love Don't Live Here

Love don't live here any more
It has long gone away
For the love that had for you
Have died from a major stab wound to the heart
Love lived here once before
But has long past away
Buried deep down in the ground
It is somewhere it will never be found
Not even a treasure
It won't bring any pleasure
For those who walks it path
Love don't live here anymore
It has long gone and passed away

The Theme of a Diva

Walking tall and strong
Is what she does
In her 5-inch heels
What name brand
We'll never know
Wearing her clothes with pride
Looking like a million bucks
Never knowing how much it cost
Holding her head up so high
She probably can touch the sky
You will never know
If she was sad, mad or just plain on glad
When she speaks
She speaks with intelligence and wisdom
Not with stupidity and ignorance
She takes pride in herself
Sporting her afro
Rocking it rough and tough
Let the young ones know
That she still got it
She walks the walk and talks the talk
Everybody can't be a diva
Many tried but few succeed
But the number one thing about a diva
Is to be successful in life

His Waters

Walking through the ran
Water dripping off my head
Trying to get the church
To hear the choir, sing my favorite song
Wearing my black brim and suede shoes
That are now drench with water
My clothes are damp
Just to think walk out the house
So fresh and so clean
As I get to the door of the Lord's house
An old lady was standing in the entrance
As I stood beside her
She asked to have you been saved
Yes, I told her
Have you been taking to his water she asks
I'm taking through the water whenever it rain, I replied
For his water is when it rains

The Married Man

My man is married to his work
He spends more time in his office than at home
He doesn't eat properly
Yesterday may have been the first descent meal
He ate in three months
He never sleeps
He stays up and works
All day and night
His eyes that was once hazel
Are now blood shot red
I told him if he doesn't slow down
That he may have a stroke
He thinks he is too young to have one
I pray to God to keep him health
But for now, I am telling him to slow down

What do you want from me

I'm not the most perfect
Woman that God let walks
The greens of this planet
I am not the brainyic that
Most people make me out to be
I am neither a bitch nor a whore
For I'm too smart
To be a whore
And have too much class
To be a super bitch
So, what do you want from me
I can cook the finest of meals
I can clean a house
To sparkle like a diamond
But do you think that
I too career orient
That I'm this so call superwoman
And the only thing that
Thrills me is power
But what do you want from me
Is it that my stomach is not as flat as a washboard
Or is it my hair is not fine or straight enough
Or my skin is not light enough
I really want to know
I can't read your mind
Can you just tell me what do want from me?

Black Panties

I lie here wearing nothing
But those lace black panties
That you love to see me in
Waiting for you to
Help me warm the sheets
I lie here ready to explore your deepest fantasies
Let me take you into your wettest dreams
Maybe we can answer the question
Why do doves cry?
Before you remove these panties
Let us get ready for our sexual journey
That will take us to a place that we never been
Come take these panties off
Miss Kitty before she throws a fit
Now you may remove the black panties

Raphael Sweet Thang

My Raphael sweet thang
A man that I swear to love for eternity
The sweetness of his voice alone
Make me wet my thong
My Raphael sweet thang
A caramel man indeed
Who hypnotize me
With those hazel eyes
Make me go into a zone
Where no other man goes
My Raphael sweet thang
With his lushes' lips
That I like to lick
With my tongue
Raphael, I will always love you
Until the sunset

Homecoming

I look down the street
To see people coming up the road
Playing songs that will lift the spirits
Behind the band are two white mustangs
Carrying a coach
Decorated in roses and baby breathe
Looking so beautiful
Riding inside is a lady
All dressed in white
She was waving at everyone
She even called some people by name
Hi Boy and Mary
Where have you been?
What's going on Alex?
Haven't visit you in a while
At the end of the road, the band disappears
The woman dressed in white
Climbs out the coach
And started climbing up the stairs
At the top is a tall man
He reached for her hand
When she gets to the top, he says
Welcome home my child

Sadness

I helped you
I gave to you
I shared with you
But what did you do?
You killed me
I worked hard for you
I tried to solve your problems
But you just want to kill me
I was even nice to you
When there is nobody to help
Or give you what gave you
You'll wish that
You haven't killed me

Make America Great Again

#45 made a statement
That he can make America great again
Well, I have some questions
That he only can answer
How are you going to make America great again?
Make America so great for the women
Who want more out life
Rather than becoming the ideal June Cleaver
And stay at home to clean the house and raise children
For the millions of immigrants
That came to this country
On the dreams of our founding fathers
What about the African American
Who was forced to come here
Enslaved for over 300 years
And spent another 50 years
Fighting for equal rights
He said that he wanted
To make America great again
But I thought that America is already great

Made in the USA
Columbia, SC
13 March 2019